GREAT ✷ SCIENTISTS

CHARLES DARWIN

WAYLAND

First published in Great Britain in 2024 by Wayland
Copyright © Hodder and Stoughton, 2024

Some of the material in this book first appeared in
Super Scientists: Charles Darwin (Watts, 2014).

Editors: Sarah Ridley and Amy Pimperton
Designer: Lisa Peacock

ISBN (HB): 978 1 5263 2646 1
ISBN (PB): 978 1 5263 2647 8

Printed and bound in Dubai

Wayland, an imprint of
Hachette Children's Group
Part of Hodder and Stoughton
Carmelite House
50 Victoria Embankment
London EC4Y 0DZ
An Hachette UK Company
www.hachette.co.uk
www.hachettechildrens.co.uk

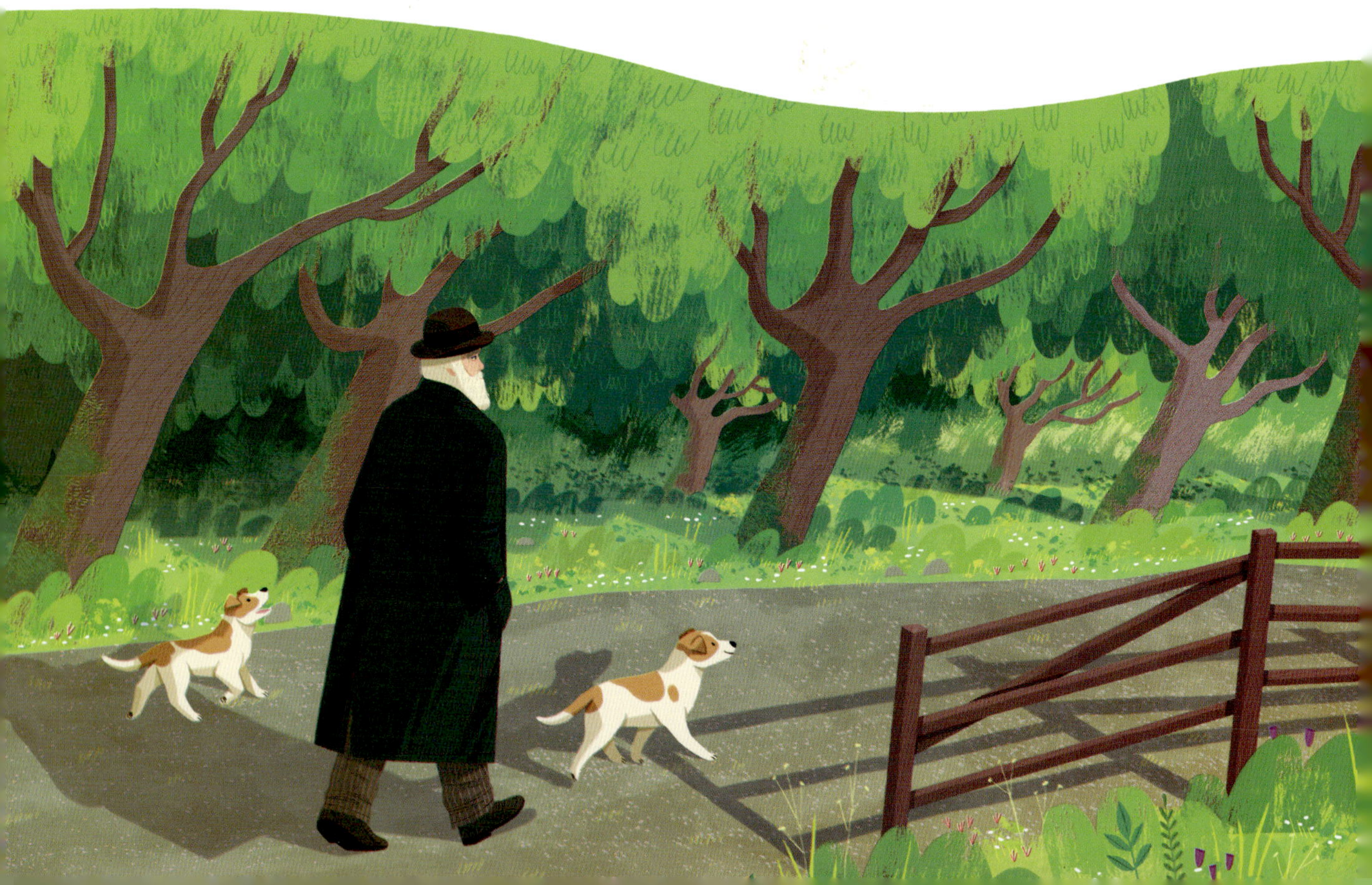

GREAT  SCIENTISTS

CHARLES DARWIN

ANNA BAKER AND ALEXANDRA BADIU

WAYLAND

Charles Darwin was born in 1809, over two hundred years ago. His father was a successful doctor and the family were wealthy. Charles lived with his brother and four sisters in a big house in Shropshire, England, called The Mount. There was always someone to play with and the family often visited cousins who lived nearby.

Sadly, Charles's mother died when he was only eight years old. Soon after, he started school, where he found many subjects boring. During the holidays, he liked to spend time in the garden and walk in the countryside. He was fascinated by nature and collected birds' eggs, plants, rocks, shells and insects.

In 1825, Charles's father sent him to Edinburgh University, Scotland, to study to become a doctor. He hated it. He couldn't stand watching operations. Instead, Charles spent most of his time studying rocks and insects. He went on trips to the countryside with his friends, collecting beetles. He labelled each one and displayed them in special boxes and drawers.

CHARLES LEARNT HOW TO TAKE NOTES AND RECORD WHAT HE SAW FROM PROFESSORS WHO WERE EXPERTS IN ROCKS, SHELLS, INSECTS AND PLANTS.

After two years, his father decided that Charles might do better as a vicar and sent him to study religious beliefs at the University of Cambridge. He graduated with his degree in 1831.

Soon after he had completed his degree, 22-year-old Charles was invited to join a long voyage. Some of his professors had recommended him to the captain of a ship. He leapt at the chance to join the team on board HMS *Beagle*. The main reason for the voyage was to map the coastline of South America. Charles's job was to study plants and animals, and to keep the captain company.

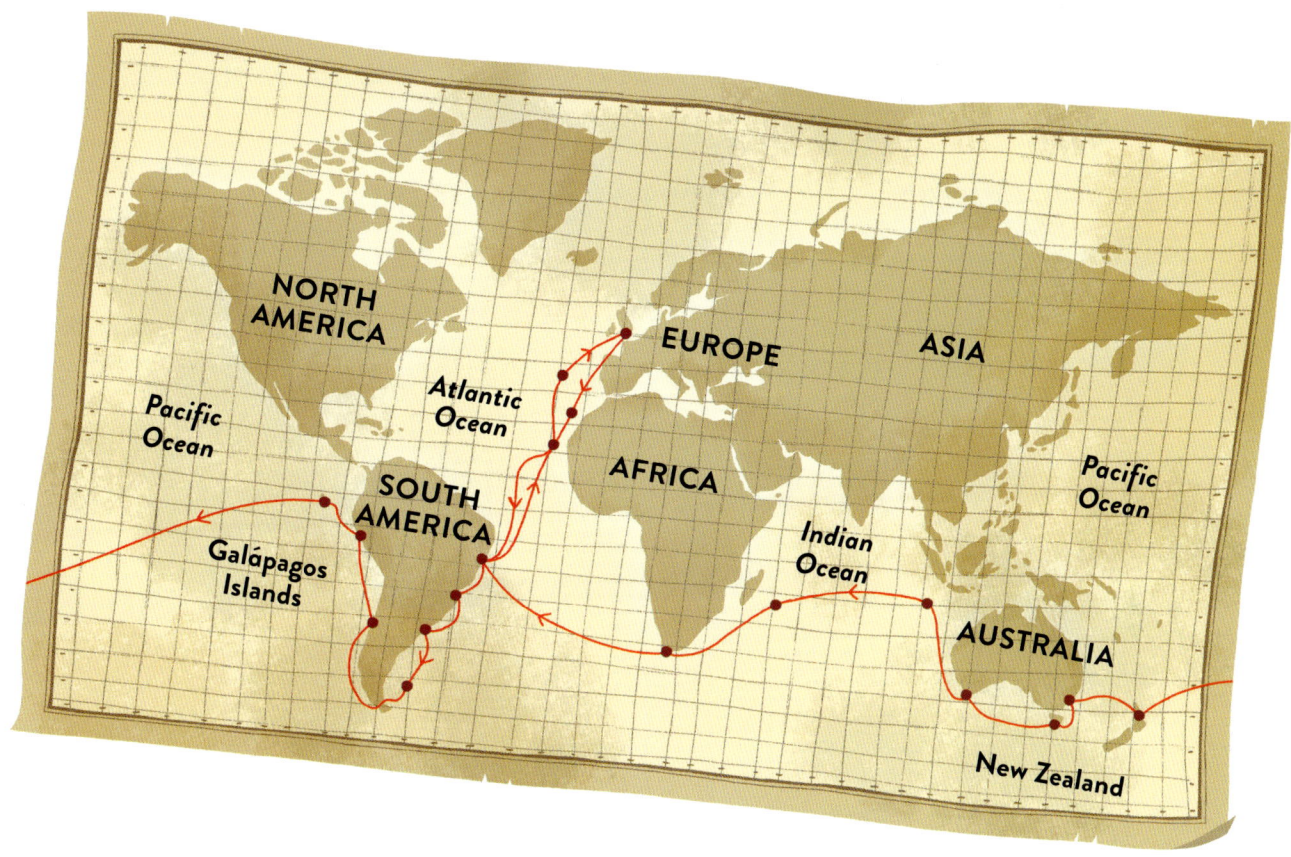

The trip was supposed to last only two years, but it took much longer than expected. Over the next five years, the ship sailed across the Atlantic Ocean to South America, sailing around the coastline and then on to the Galápagos Islands. From there it journeyed to New Zealand, Australia, around the tip of southern Africa and back to England.

Out at sea, Charles felt very seasick. When he felt better, he read a book written by a geologist called Charles Lyell. In Charles Darwin's time, many people thought that God created the world in six days, about 6,000 years earlier. Lyell, however, believed that Earth was millions of years old because of the evidence contained in ancient fossils and rocks. Lyell's book gave Charles Darwin many new ideas about how Earth formed.

Off the west coast of Africa, Charles spotted a band of crushed seashells in a cliff high above the sea. How had the shells of dead sea creatures ended up there? He collected rocks, shells and fossils, and recorded where he found them in his notebooks.

The ship sailed on to Brazil, South America. While other members of the crew mapped the coastline, Charles explored the rainforest. He was amazed by the variety of animals and plants he saw there.

He watched leaf-cutter ants as they marched along their trails in the rainforest.

He collected specimens of many different sorts of plant, including orchids. He was amazed by the colourful birds, including hummingbirds and toucans.

He collected lizards, beetles and butterflies.

He described what he saw in hundreds of letters to family and friends back in England, including university professors.

The HMS *Beagle* sailed on along the coast of South America. In Argentina, guides helped him to find the plants, animals and fossils he wanted to collect. He found the fossil of a huge armadillo-like creature called a glyptodont. He realised its armoured skin, claws and teeth were similar to the much smaller armadillos he saw living in the grasslands. He wondered how this could be.

Armadillo

Glyptodont

When they reached the Galápagos Islands, Charles saw incredible reptiles, such as giant tortoises and marine iguanas.

His assistant, Syms Covington, helped Charles
to collect and preserve the plant and animal
specimens in different ways, including drying
them out, cleaning up skeletons
and placing them in jars.

After the Galápagos Islands, they sailed on to New Zealand and Australia. In October 1836, after almost five years away, HMS *Beagle* finally arrived back in England. They had survived storms and an earthquake, as well as very hot and very cold weather.

Charles set to work sorting out his notes and his specimens. Experts helped him and took a great interest in what he had found. He kept returning to what he had learnt and collected during his voyage on the HMS *Beagle*.

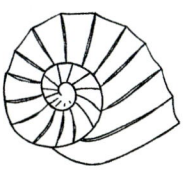

IN 1837, CHARLES SKETCHED THE OUTLINE OF A BIG NEW IDEA. HE CALLED IT 'THE TREE OF LIFE'.

Charles's idea was a new kind of family tree linking all living animals and plants – as well as species that had died out – with one shared ancestor. He believed that species' had changed (evolved) over time, but he worried that people would not understand this theory. For now, he decided to write about it in secret notebooks. He only discussed the idea with his closest friends – Charles Lyell, who he became friends with on his return to London, and Joseph Hooker.

In 1839, Charles married his cousin, Emma Wedgwood.

At first, they lived in London. Three years later
they moved to a beautiful house in the countryside.
It was a perfect place for them to bring up their large
family. In time, they had ten children together.

Charles loved family life, but also spent hours every day researching, experimenting and writing. He bred pigeons and rabbits and joined groups of breeders to exchange ideas with them. He saw how breeders chose to breed certain pigeons together to produce varieties of pigeon with different coloured beaks or feathers, for instance. Understanding selective breeding helped Charles develop his ideas about natural selection (see next page).

Out in his garden and greenhouses, Charles carried out many experiments with plants.

When he had returned from his earlier travels, Charles gave a collection of the bird and animal specimens from his trip to the Natural History Museum in London, England. A bird expert at the museum, called John Gould, showed Charles that some small birds collected from the Galápagos Islands were all finches.

Charles gradually worked out that each species of finch had been collected from a different island and that the shape of their beak helped them find food available there.

Charles realised that over generations, finches with beaks that gave them a better chance of finding food passed on this advantage to their own chicks. Over many generations, these tiny variations in beak size became bigger and eventually resulted in a new species. From one ancestor, 13 different species of finch had evolved. He called this idea 'evolution by natural selection'.

Charles continued to study and research his ideas about evolution, but he wasn't ready to tell everyone about these ideas. However, he did write several science books on other topics. This was all to change when he received a letter from the naturalist Alfred Russel Wallace in 1858, describing his ideas about evolution by natural selection. Charles was stunned as they matched his own ideas about evolution.

Alfred Russel Wallace went on many research trips around the world. When he wrote to Charles, he was studying the wildlife of islands in Malaysia.

Charles decided that the fair thing to do was to present both their ideas to the Linnean Society. Its members were an important group of scientists and natural historians. However, neither Alfred nor Charles attended the meeting. Alfred was travelling and, sadly, one of Charles's children had died.

Charles realised that he must publish his own work on evolution – and quickly! He set his ideas down in a short book called *On the Origin of Species* and it was published in 1859. Bookshops ran out of copies on the first day.

Charles's book, *On the Origin of Species*, upset many people. Religious people who believed that God had created all animals and plants as we see them today disagreed with Charles's theory. Newspapers published stories for and against his ideas. Scientists and thinkers discussed the book at meetings. The book sold thousands of copies and made Charles famous.

Charles spent most of the rest of his life enjoying time at home and the peace of his garden and the countryside. He also carried on his research and experiments. These led to more books about plants, animals and evolution. He took daily walks along a sandy path close to his home, which he named 'my thinking path'.

Charles's interest in the natural world continued up to his death. At the end of his life he was fascinated by worms and the way they recycle dead plant material into the soil.

In 1882, Charles died at home, surrounded by his family. He was 73. His funeral was held in Westminster Abbey, London, England, and attended by many important people.

In 1885, there was a grand ceremony when a large statue of Charles Darwin went on show at the Natural History Museum in London, England, to celebrate this great scientist.

If you visit the Natural History Museum, you can see the statue today.

TIMELINE

1809 Charles Darwin was born.

1815 Charles's mother, Susannah, died.

1816 Charles and his elder brother, Erasmus, attended the local public school.

1825 Charles and Erasmus were sent to Edinburgh University to study medicine.

1826 Charles joined the Plinian Society at Edinburgh University, for students interested in natural history.

1827 Charles left Edinburgh University after two years without achieving his degree. He then attended Cambridge University to study religious beliefs.

1831 Charles graduated from Cambridge University. He joined the HMS *Beagle* on an expedition to map the coastline of South America.

1832–1835 Charles read Charles Lyell's book, *Principles of Geology* and observed the geology of the West African coastline. The HMS *Beagle* sailed on to Brazil, and then around South America. Charles collected specimens and wrote many letters about his finds. He found a glyptodont fossil in Argentina.

1835 The HMS *Beagle* arrived at the Galápagos Islands. Charles recorded what he saw, including several species of bird. He collected many more specimens.

1835–1836 The HMS *Beagle* sailed to New Zealand and Australia and then back to England, via the tip of Southern Africa.

1836 Charles and Charles Lyell met for the first time.

1837 Charles moved to London. His Galápagos birds were studied by the English ornithologist, John Gould, who showed Charles that these birds were all finches. This inspired Charles's theory of 'evolution by natural selection'. Charles worked on his 'tree of life' theory.

1839 Charles married his cousin, Emma Wedgwood. He published a book called *The Voyage of the Beagle*.

1842 Charles and Emma moved to Down House in Kent where Charles continued to work on his theories.

1858 The naturalist, Alfred Russel Wallace, wrote to Charles with his own ideas about evolution by natural selection. Charles Lyell and Joseph Hooker presented both Charles's and Alfred's theories to the Linnean Society on behalf of both men.

1859 Charles published *On the Origin of Species*. It upset many religious people. Thousands more copies were sold and Charles became famous.

1871 Charles published another controversial book called *The Descent of Man*.

1882 Charles Darwin died aged 73. He was buried at Westminster Abbey in the Scientists' Corner, close to other famous scientists, including Isaac Newton and his friend, Charles Lyell.

QUIZ

1. What was Charles's family home called?

2. What did Charles prefer to do instead of studying for his degree in medicine at Edinburgh University?

3. What was the name of the ship that Charles was invited to join for an expedition?

4. What was the main aim of the expedition?

5. In Argentina, Charles found a fossil of a glyptodont. What animal living today is it similar to?

6. What species of bird did Charles find on the Galápagos Islands?

7. What was the name of the naturalist who was also working on a theory of evolution by natural selection?

8. What was Charles's famous book about evolution by natural selection called?

9. What did Charles call the sandy path close to his home that he took daily walks on?

10. Where is Charles buried?

The answers are on page 32.

GLOSSARY

ancestor An individual that has died, and from whom other individuals are descended.

armoured Covered with a protective layer.

evolution The process of change over time.

fossil The trace of an animal or plant, preserved in rock.

Galápagos Islands A group of 19 main islands and many islets (small islands) that are part of Ecuador.

HMS Stands for His/Her Majesty's Ship.

Linnean Society A society devoted to natural history, which is the study of animals and plants, and the whole of the natural world, including palaeontology (the study of fossils).

natural selection How individual living things that are best suited to where they live are more likely to survive and pass on any natural advantage to their offspring.

preserve To keep something as it is, rather than letting it decay.

professor A high-ranking teacher at a university.

selective breeding When an animal breeder chooses which individuals to breed together, to produce offspring with certain qualities. For example, a racing pigeon breeder may choose to breed together a very fast pigeon with a very intelligent pigeon.

species A group of similar living things that share a name and are able to breed with one another.

specimen A single plant or animal, for example, that is used for scientific study or display.

theory A set of ideas that aim to explain something.

voyage A long sea (or space) journey.

INDEX

Quiz answers: 1. The Mount; 2. study rocks and insects, and collect beetles; 3. HMS *Beagle*; 4. to map the coastline of South America; 5. armadillo; 6. finch; 7. Alfred Russel Wallace; 8. *On the Origin of Species*; 9. 'my thinking path'; 10. Westminster Abbey.